# Amazing
# Grace and Flavour

## Michael Smith

BRITISH BROADCASTING CORPORATION

Cover photo by Michael Boys

The dishes in the photo are Crown of Lamb with
Rice Pilaf, Apple Butter Cream, Chocolate
Gooseberry Cake, and Chilled Red Pimento and
Ginger Soup.

Published by the British Broadcasting Corporation,
35 Marylebone High Street, London W1M 4AA
ISBN 0 563 20189 4
First published 1983   Reprinted 1983
© Michael Smith 1983

Set in 10/11 pt Times New Roman
by Ace Filmsetting Ltd, Frome, Somerset
and printed in England by
R. J. Acford Ltd, Chichester, Sussex.

# Contents

**Menu Seven**
Buttered Eggs in a Shell  34
Glazed Loin of Pork  35
Braised Red Cabbage  59
Chocolate and Gooseberry Cake  37

**Menu Eight**
Avocado Salad with *Foie Gras* and Tarragon  39
Broccoli and Lobster Flan  40
Norwegian Cream  41

**Menu Nine**
Minestrone  43
Stuffed Boned Capon  45
Tomato Madeira Sauce  46
Gooseberry Fool with Rose-flower Water  48

**Menu Ten**
Eggs with Avocado and Watercress Mayonnaise  49
Old English Duck Pie with Forcemeat Balls and
Chestnuts  50
Fig 'Sue'  51

**Menu Eleven**
Chilled Cream of Tomato Soup with Turmeric,
Orange and Shrimps  52
Cold Pâté Stuffed Duck  53
Orange Soufflé (Hot)  54

**Menu Twelve**
Chilled Pea, Mint and Lemon Soup with Soured
Cream  56
Beef and Red Pepper Sauce (to serve with pasta)  57
Apple Butter Creams  58

A Selection of Vegetables and Salads  59

# Introduction

Writing about rich food during a recession at first gave me a feeling of guilt; how can one justify spending hard-earned money on butter, cream, wines, elaborate cuts of meat and even pâté de foie gras, which I call for in one recipe in this book? However, we all know that it is a *great* deal cheaper to wine and dine our guests at home than it is to take them out to a restaurant where even a simple pizza and bottle of house plonk for two people cuts into a £10 note.

Another argument for dining well at home is that of personal priorities: hair-dos, sports centres, golf and the new cult of aerobic classes all slot into the category of leisure-spending and are certainly not necessities. They are, however, good for the soul! Gourmet cooking too can help boost your spirits and a luscious menu need not cost any more than the aforesaid luxuries. Take the cost of any one of the average simple weekly hobbies and you'll soon top the cost of a pint of cream or a splash of sherry to enhance the sauce on a piece of salmon or tender breast of a farm-reared chicken.

Cooking, particularly for those who don't have to prepare three family meals daily, is fast becoming a hobby, for men as well as women. Here in this book, I have suggested a series of twelve menus, not necessarily to be cooked in the order they appear, but for you to dip into and chop and change at will, forming your own 'marriage' of dishes. The separate list of unusual ways of serving salads and vegetables is there for you to add to your chosen main course.

*Michael Smith 1983*

## Conversion Tables

All these are approximate conversions which have either been rounded up or down. Never mix imperial and metric measures in one recipe, stick to one system or the other.

*Oven temperature*

| Mark 1 | 275°F | 140°C |
|---|---|---|
| 2 | 300° | 150° |
| 3 | 325° | 170° |
| 4 | 350° | 180° |
| 5 | 375° | 190° |
| 6 | 400° | 200° |
| 7 | 425° | 220° |
| 8 | 450° | 230° |
| 9 | 475° | 240° |

*Volume*

| 2 fl oz | 55 ml |
|---|---|
| 3 | 75 |
| 5 ($\frac{1}{4}$ pt) | 150 |
| $\frac{1}{2}$ pt | 275 |
| $\frac{3}{4}$ | 425 |
| 1 | 570 |
| $1\frac{3}{4}$ | 1 litre |

*Measurements*

| $\frac{1}{8}$ inch | 3 mm |
|---|---|
| $\frac{1}{4}$ | $\frac{1}{2}$ cm |
| $\frac{1}{2}$ | 1 |
| $\frac{3}{4}$ | 2 |
| 1 | 2.5 |
| $1\frac{1}{4}$ | 3 |
| $1\frac{1}{2}$ | 4 |
| $1\frac{3}{4}$ | 4.5 |
| 2 | 5 |
| 3 | 7.5 |
| 4 | 10 |
| 5 | 13 |
| 6 | 15 |
| 7 | 18 |
| 8 | 20 |
| 9 | 23 |
| 10 | 25.5 |
| 11 | 28 |
| 12 | 30 |

*Weights*

| $\frac{1}{2}$ oz | 10 g |
|---|---|
| 1 | 25 |
| $1\frac{1}{2}$ | 40 |
| 2 | 50 |
| $2\frac{1}{2}$ | 60 |
| 3 | 75 |
| 4 | 110 |
| $4\frac{1}{2}$ | 125 |
| 5 | 150 |
| 6 | 175 |
| 7 | 200 |
| 8 | 225 |
| 9 | 250 |
| 10 | 275 |
| 12 | 350 |
| 1 lb | 450 |
| $1\frac{1}{2}$ | 700 |
| 2 | 900 |
| 3 | 1 kg 350 g |

# MENU 1

Oeufs en Gelée au Mousse de Foie Gras
Boiled Ribs of Beef with Caper
and Chive Sauce
Black Forest Cake

### *Oeufs en Gelée au Mousse de Foie Gras*

This is a recipe where cheating is essential: for one cannot think that even a purist could find the time, energy and professional know-how to produce a result as acceptable as the one I give here for this rich exotic starter.

This is also an ideal dish for an exotic formal picnic.

6 *oeufs mollets* (cold, soft boiled eggs)
1 × 4 oz tin of *mousse de foie gras* or Swiss *parfait*, chilled
2 tins good consommé such as Baxters, Crosse & Blackwell

1 sachet gelatine crystals
2 tsp. lemon juice
1 tbsp snipped chives and/or chopped parsley

Measure one pint of consommé into a pan (drink the remainder) and add the lemon juice. Bring to boiling point. Remove from heat, sprinkle over the gelatine crystals, stir until dissolved. Leave to cool but not set.

An *oeuf mollet* to me is approximately a 6-minute egg: soft in the middle and the white still soft.

Shell the eggs carefully under cold running water.

Open the *mousse de foie gras* at both ends and push the block out. Cut into six even-sized slices. Put one slice in the bottom of a number 3 ramekin, cocotte or pretty tea-cup. The receptacle needs to be fairly deep to contain the egg which you now sit on top of the pâté.

Sprinkle with the herbs. Ladle over enough of the cold consommé to just cover. Put to set.

Eat with a teaspoon accompanied by hot dry toast, cheese shortbreads or plain crackers.

This recipe is excellent when made with quails' eggs, in which case allow three eggs per serving, cooking them in gently boiling water for 2–3 minutes. Serves 6


## Boiled Ribs of Beef with Caper and Chive Sauce

When one thinks of boiled beef and carrots with caper sauce, memories of robust meals from our grand-parents' table spring to mind.

Try my way of cooking this English dish. The meat will (or should) be tender and succulent: the sauce is rich, yet light, spicy and flavourful. The quality of the dish will always depend on the quality of the meat purchased. It should not be a sin to boil *ribs* of beef: to boil this cut of beef should be a late twentieth-century virtue.

| | |
|---|---|
| 1 × 5–6 lb rib of beef, boned, rolled and tied | 1 bay leaf* |
| | 2 tsp salt* |
| 1 bottle dry white wine* | 12 peppercorns* |
| 1 onion* | Boiling water |
| 1 carrot* | 6 medium carrots |
| 1 sprig thyme (or level tsp dried)* | 6 leeks |
| | 1 cauliflower |

In a pan just large enough to contain the beef, bring the wine to the boil and add the asterisked ingredients. Put in the beef. Add boiling water, just to cover. Cook the beef very gently for 1½ hours.

Remove the beef to a warm serving platter and cover with a damp cloth. Boil the carrots and leeks in the stock until tender. (Cook the cauliflower or any other vegetables you may wish to serve separately in another pan.)

Strain the stock through a sieve lined with a clean cotton handkerchief. (Many people say strain through kitchen paper, but this takes for ever!)

*Sauce*
2 oz butter
1 tsp flour
¾ pt double cream
Juice of half a small
  lemon (about 1 tbsp)

3 oz plump capers
1 bunch chives, chopped
1 pint stock (from
  the boiled beef)

Melt the butter in a heavy-bottomed pan, stir in the modicum of flour, pour in the stock, bring to boiling point and add the cream. Simmer over a low heat for 20–30 minutes, by which time the sauce will have reduced to about ¾ pint. Check the seasoning and add the lemon juice. Add the capers and chives. Serves 6–8

**Black Forest Cake**

6 oz unsalted butter,
  softened
6 oz moist brown sugar
  (not Demerara)
1 tbsp Golden Syrup
4 oz self-raising flour,
  sieved with

2 oz cocoa and 1 level
  tsp baking powder
3 eggs, beaten
1 tbsp Maraschino,
  Kirsch or Brandy

*Fillings*

2 × 8 oz tins Morello
   cherries, pitted
1 tsp arrowroot, slaked
   in a little of the
   cherry tin juice

1 pt double cream
   whipped with 1 oz
   icing sugar and 2 fl oz
   Maraschino or Kirsch
   or Brandy

*Garnish*

1 × 6 oz block Bournville
   chocolate, chilled,
   then grated and
   chilled again

Extra whipped cream
Maraschino cherries or
   Glacé cherries

Butter and line with buttered papers three 7 inch diameter sponge tins. Cream butter and sugar until light and fluffy. Beat in the syrup.

Gradually beat in the eggs, adding a sprinkling of the flour mixture as you go along. Add the tablespoon of the Maraschino, Kirsch or Brandy.

Cut and fold in the rest of the flour and cocoa. The mixture should be of a soft dropping consistency. If not, add a spoonful of cold water.

Divide the mixture between the three tins. Level the tops. Bake at Gas Mark 5, 375°F for 20–25 minutes, or until risen and resistant to a light press with a finger.

Leave to cool for a minute or two, then turn the cakes onto cooling racks. Leave to cool completely.

Bring the juice from the cherries to the boil, whisk in enough of the slaked arrowroot to thicken this (until it is the consistency of custard).

Leave to cool, then just pour enough over the cherries to bind them.

To make up the gâteau splash a little liqueur over each cake. Place the first cake on a cake-board. Spread with the cherry mixture to the edges. Place the second cake on top. Spread evenly with one-third of the whipped cream, icing sugar and liqueur mixture.

Place the third cake on top, spread with a thinner layer of the cream, then spread the remaining cream round the sides.

Gently press the grated chocolate round the sides and sprinkle over the top. Decorate with blobs of cream, and Maraschino cherries.

Chill for an hour or so. (This cake will freeze very well.) Serves 6–8

# MENU 2

*Chilled Red Pimento and Ginger Soup*
*Roast Duckling with Walnut, Apricot*
*and Raisin Stuffing*
*Banana and Chestnut Vacherin*

**Chilled Red Pimento and Ginger Soup**

4 red peppers
2 large leeks
4 oz butter*
2 level tsp ground ginger*
2 heaped tsp sweet
  paprika*
1 oz castor sugar*
1 tsp salt*
1 tsp freshly milled white
  pepper*

Zest and juice of 1 large
  orange*
1 pt chicken stock
1 pt buttermilk
$\frac{1}{4}$ pt double cream
1 green pepper
2 pieces stem ginger

Soften without browning the leeks and red peppers
in the butter. Add all the asterisked ingredients and
stock and simmer for 30 minutes. Cool. Then with a
food processor or 'mouli' blend to a fine purée,
preferably rubbing the soup through a sieve as well.
Chill well. Stir in the buttermilk. Chill again. 'Marble'
each serving with cream.

Garnish with thin striplets of stem ginger and
striplets of green pepper. Serves 6

## Roast Duckling with Walnut, Apricot and Raisin Stuffing

1 duck (4–5 lb)
1 onion, chopped
½ small head of celery
  – knife-shredded
2 oz butter
6 oz walnuts, pulverised
  or roughly crushed*
6 oz dried apricots, diced*
1 clove garlic, crushed*
4 oz seedless raisins,
  whole*

Level tsp salt*
Level tsp black pepper*
Grated rind and juice of
  1 orange*
Grated rind and juice of
  1 small lemon*
2 carrots, sliced
1 onion, sliced
2 sticks celery, chopped
1 tomato, quartered

The texture of this recipe can be changed – made rougher or smoother – by adjusting the texture of the walnuts. If you like the walnuts crunchy, halve the quantity of orange juice.

Soften the onion and celery in the butter in a pan over a low heat. Cool. Combine the asterisked ingredients with the softened onion and celery and pack into the duck. Lay the duck in a roasting tin on a bed of carrots, the onion, the celery and the tomato. Roast at Gas Mark 6, 400°F for about 1½–2 hours or until the juices run clear.

This stuffing recipe makes enough for 2 small ducklings or 1 large duck. Serves 5–6

*To make a good duck gravy*
Carefully decant away all excess fats from the roasting tin, holding back any dark juices and residues. Sprinkle over this a good teaspoon of flour and work it well in, using a straight-edged wooden spatula.

Place the tin over a medium heat and let everything brown a little more if the vegetable mixture is not already well browned. Work it well in with the spatula.

Pour in 4 fluid ounces of Amontillado sherry.

Crumble in a chicken stock cube, then add $\frac{3}{4}$ pint of cold water. Bring everything to the boil, lower the heat and simmer for 3–4 minutes. Now strain everything through a fine-meshed strainer into a small pan.

Reduce this gravy or sauce to half a pint by boiling rapidly. It will now be shiny or glossy, and hey presto! you'll have the best and brightest duck gravy in the land. Serves 5–6

### Banana and Chestnut Vacherin

Actually this recipe resembles a Pavlova in format and you may well call it by its 'down-under' name.

| | |
|---|---|
| 4 oz egg whites | $\frac{1}{2}$ tsp vanilla essence |
| 8 oz castor sugar | 1 tsp wine vinegar (white) |
| 1 level tsp cornflour | |

Line a baking tray with silicone paper. Mark out with a pencil two 10 inch circles, or one huge oblong or square.

Beat the egg whites, preferably with an electric whisk, until they just stand in stiff peaks. Beat in half the sugar, the cornflour, vinegar and vanilla essence. Beat again until stiff. Cut and fold in the remaining sugar.

Spoon onto the baking sheet spreading lightly to your chosen shape. Bake at Gas Mark 3, 325°F for $1\frac{1}{4}$ hours. Turn the heat off and leave the vacherins in the oven until cold. They should be crisp on the exterior and somewhat gooey inside.

*Filling*

| | |
|---|---|
| $\frac{3}{4}$ pt double cream | 2 tbsp liqueur (Cointreau, |
| 2 oz castor sugar | Drambuie, Curaçao) |
| 1 tsp vanilla essence | 2 bananas |

Juice of 1 lemon
8 oz tin chestnuts in
  syrup (or any exotic
  fruits if chestnuts are
  not available)

4 oz grated chocolate
2 oz toasted flaked
  almonds
1 tbsp icing sugar

*To make up the vacherin*
You have the alternative of making a 'lidded' vacherin
or an open-faced one. First, slice the bananas and toss
in the lemon juice. Then mix the vanilla essence, the
liqueur with the cream and castor sugar and beat until
stiff.

Pipe a deep collar of the whipped cream round the
edges and arrange the bananas and the chestnuts
inside the collar. Sprinkle with the chocolates and
almonds.

If you make a lidded vacherin, sit the second
vacherin on top and dredge the whole with icing sugar.
Serves 6–8

# MENU 3

*Creamy Chicken Soup with Smoked Salmon*
*Roast Crown of Lamb with Pilaf Rice Stuffing*
*Chocolate Chip Sponge Pudding*
*with Redcurrant Coulis and Soured Cream*

**Creamy Chicken Soup with Smoked Salmon**

The marriage of whisky and smoked foods is excellent and makes this a very unusual soup for serving at a special dinner party.

1½ pt hot chicken stock
(See pp. 23–4 or use
   stock cube)
2 oz French or Dutch
   unsalted butter
1½ oz plain white flour

⅓ pt double cream
1 sherry glassful whisky
1 egg yolk
Salt and freshly milled
   pepper if necessary

*Garnish*
1 chicken breast cut into
   striplets

2 oz smoked salmon cut
   into strips, or rolled
   and cut into rings

Melt the butter slowly in a heavy-bottomed pan. Do not allow it to get too hot or it will add a nutty flavour to the soup which in some soups is desirable but not in this one.

Stir in the flour, add the stock whisking as you go along.

Allow the soup to simmer for 10 minutes to ensure

the flour is 'cooked out' and has done its thickening job. Add the cream. Season. Just before serving, put equal amounts of the garnish into warm soup cups. Whisk the egg yolk with the whisky in a large bowl. Bring the soup to the bowl and strain into the bowl whisking well to incorporate the whisky and yolk mixture.

Ladle immediately into the soup cups.

Once the yolk has been added the soup should not boil again or the yolk will curdle. Serves 4

## Roast Crown of Lamb with Pilaf Rice Stuffing

1 crown of lamb
  (12–14 bones)

*Savoury butter*

| | |
|---|---|
| 2 cloves garlic, crushed | 1 tsp salt |
| Level tsp ground rosemary | 1 tsp milled pepper |
| | 1 tsp grated lemon rind |
| Level tsp ground bay | 4 oz softened butter |

Mix all the ingredients to a smooth paste. Spread inside and outside the crown.

Cover tips with foil. Roast in a pre-heated oven at Gas Mark 9, 475°F for 30 minutes. Reduce the temperature to Gas Mark 6, 400°F for a further 30 minutes (or longer if you like lamb well done).

Fill with the following stuffing just before serving:

| | |
|---|---|
| 8 oz long grain rice | 1 medium onion, finely chopped |
| 20 fl oz rich chicken stock (2 stock cubes) | 1 clove garlic, crushed |
| 2 sticks celery, finely diced | 4 oz green gammon (raw ham) finely diced |
| 4 oz mushrooms, chopped | 2 oz butter |

| 4 oz freshly grated | Salt and milled pepper |
| Parmesan cheese | $\frac{1}{4}$ tsp ground thyme |
| 3 oz extra unsalted | 2 oz toasted almonds |
| butter, softened | |

Pre-heat the oven to Gas Mark 7, 425°F. Melt half the butter (1 ounce) in a heavy-bottomed pan. Fry the ham until cooked. With a draining spoon remove to an oven-proof casserole.

Add the remaining butter (1 ounce) to the pan and over a gentle heat soften the onion and celery. Add the rice and fry this for a minute or so, adding the mushrooms as you stir.

Turn all of this mixture into the casserole. Mix in the crushed garlic and a smidge of ground thyme (about $\frac{1}{4}$ tsp).

Salt and pepper lightly (this will depend how salty the stock and ham are, so taste everything in due course). Bring the stock to the boil. Pour over the rice and stir well. Put a lid on the casserole and cook in the oven for 20–25 minutes, after which time all the liquid will have been absorbed and the rice just cooked.

With a fork, mix in the extra softened butter and grated cheese. Pile the pilaf into the centre of the crown. Sprinkle with the toasted almonds. Serve any remaining pilaf in a warm tureen. The pilaf is to be seen as taking the place of potatoes.

Serves 6–8 depending on the size of the crown.

*Note*
I have been served many a splendiferous crown of lamb. A deal of work has gone into the preparation and presentation of this handsome dish, but often the roast has been spoiled as the fat inside is undercooked.

To me, stuffing a crown-roast is a folly. How can the searing heat, necessary to seal and crisp a good roast, get at the lamb fat when the stuffing is *in situ*?

I always advise people to roast the crown on its own.

Choose a stuffing like the one I give here, which can be cooked separately and spooned into the centre at the last moment leaving the fat crisp, succulent and flavoursome and the nugget of sweet meat deliciously pink.

I think a pilaf and lamb marry well and are moist enough without gravy. If you feel you would like to serve a sauce, then the tomato sauce on p. 46 would be very good with it.

## Chocolate Chip Sponge Pudding with Redcurrant Coulis and Soured Cream

This dark-toned but light and fluffy sponge pudding is not to be restricted to the colder months any more than a soufflé. It is lighter textured than many a summer pudding I've had!

*Redcurrant Coulis*

| | |
|---|---|
| 1 lb fresh or frozen redcurrants | 2 oz (or less) castor sugar Juice of one lemon |

Toss all the ingredients together in a pan over a low heat until the juices draw. Press and rub through a fine sieve. Chill well.

*Pudding*

| | |
|---|---|
| 2 large eggs, beaten | Cold water |
| 4 oz unsalted butter | 2 oz bitter chocolate, crushed to $\frac{1}{4}$ in. chips |
| 4 oz castor sugar | |
| 2 tsp vanilla essence | $\frac{1}{3}$ pt sour cream (optional) |
| 4 oz plain white flour – sifted twice together with 2 oz cocoa powder and 2 heaped tsp baking powder | |

Well butter a 1½-pint basin or mould.

Cream butter and sugar until light and fluffy. Add vanilla essence. Gradually beat in the eggs: if they show signs of 'splitting' or 'curdling' add a small spoonful of the flour mixture.

Cut and fold in thoroughly the remaining flour mixture using a little cold water to arrive at a loose dropping consistency. (This means that the mixture drops away from the spoon or spatula as soon as it is held up from the bowl with no pause in between.) Mix in the chocolate chips.

Spoon into the buttered basin. Level the top. Cover with buttered foil. Make a pleat to allow the pudding to rise. Tie down with string. Steam over water boiling at a steady roll for 1½ hours. Turn out and serve immediately with the chilled (or hot) redcurrant sauce and soured cream.

In the summer, instead of chocolate chips I scatter in a small carton of fresh redcurrants, which creates great excitement among my guests! Serves 5–6

# MENU 4

Eggs Tabbouleh
Chicken Vol-au-Vent with Asparagus
and 'Oyster' Mushrooms
Pears in Sauternes, with Orange Rum Sabayon

**Eggs Tabbouleh**

Burghul, or cracked wheat as it is known in our health food shops, is delicious and as a salad mixed with spring onions, parsley and the all-essential mint, goes well with cold lamb or chicken. Here I have piled it onto half, lightly hard-boiled eggs.

8 hard-boiled eggs
8 oz cracked wheat
Cold chicken stock to cover (use cube)
2 tomatoes, skinned, de-seeded and chopped
1 bunch spring onions, trimmed but the green left on and finely chopped
1 teacup freshly chopped parsley
1 teacup freshly chopped mint
$\frac{1}{4}$ pt good olive oil
1 tbsp wine vinegar
Juice of one large lemon
2 level tsps *mild* French mustard
Salt and milled black pepper

Soak the wheat for an hour in the cold stock (if you are a vegetarian use cold water). It will swell. Drain, and squeeze out surplus moisture. Spread the soaked wheat on a clean tea towel to dry a little.

Mix the oil, mustard and vinegar together. To this mixture, add everything else except the eggs and place in a large bowl. Cover and refrigerate until ready for use.

Cut the eggs in half lengthways; remove the yolks. Fill the eggs until piled up, with Tabbouleh. Arrange in a dish. Push the yolks through a hair sieve and sprinkle over the filled eggs.

### Chicken *Vol-au-Vent* with Asparagus and 'Oyster' Mushrooms

2 × 12 oz packets of
  frozen puff pastry
1 egg, beaten
1 × 4 lb chicken, boiled
12 spears of fresh
  asparagus, cooked and
  kept warm with the
  chicken

8 oz 'oyster' mushrooms
  or ordinary large,
  white caps, quartered

Thaw the pastry.

On a well-floured surface, carefully and *evenly* roll each block of pastry into even-sized rectangles approximately 10 inches × 6 inches. (Using a ruler, cut each to the same size.)

Place the first rectangle on a wetted baking sheet. Brush all over with beaten egg, avoiding getting any egg on the side edges as this will inhibit the rising of the pastry.

Carefully cut out a rectangular piece from the second rolled block of pastry, leaving a border about 1 inch broad.

Lift this border and lay it on the egg-washed pastry on the baking tray. Press down gently. Brush the top of the border with egg.

Bake the oblong piece of pastry removed from the

centre, alongside the *vol-au-vent*. Bake in a pre-heated oven, Gas Mark 8, 450°F for 20 minutes. Lower the temperature to Gas Mark 5, 375°F for a further 20 minutes. Remove the *vol-au-vent* from the oven and carefully cut out and scrape away any risen pastry from the centre oblong cavity. Lower the temperature to Gas Mark 3, 325°F and return the shell to the oven to dry out and get crisp right through. This will take another 15 minutes. The pastry must be crisp, dry and golden-brown.

The 'lid' should be fine by now, but if it shows a tendency to be undercooked, leave it in the oven.

If your particular oven starts to scorch the pastry, you must obviously lower the temperature according- ly. It should be quite brittle. Don't worry if it hasn't risen evenly, it will still taste good.

The *vol-au-vent* can be made two or three days earlier and warmed through with the chicken (q.v.) at Gas Mark $\frac{1}{2}$, 100°F.

*To boil the chicken*

| | |
|---|---|
| 1 × 4 lb chicken | 12 peppercorns* |
| 1 onion, quartered* | 1 × 2 in. piece lemon rind* |
| 2 sticks celery, cut up* | 2 tsp·salt* |
| 2 carrots, peeled and cut up* | Enough water and $\frac{1}{2}$ pt dry white wine to cover* |
| 1 bouquet of herbs* | |
| 1 extra bay leaf* | |

Bring all the asterisked ingredients to the boil. Lower the chicken into a pan just large enough to contain it together with the vegetables. The liquid should just cover it.

Bring back to the boil and cook at a very gentle roll for $1\frac{1}{4}$ hours, when the chicken should be cooked but still succulent. Try it, by pulling the leg away from the body: it should just come away without resistance. (Experience helps here!)

23

Remove the chicken. Strain the stock into a clean pan. Leave for 15 minutes for the fats to come to the surface. Skim these off and discard.

Skin, bone and cut the chicken flesh into bite-sized pieces, put to keep warm in a lidded casserole in the oven at Gas Mark $\frac{1}{2}$, 100°F whilst you make the sauce.

*Sauce*

| | |
|---|---|
| 2 oz butter | 5 fl oz Amontillado-type |
| 1$\frac{1}{2}$ oz plain white flour | sherry |
| $\frac{3}{4}$ pt chicken stock (q.v.) | Salt if necessary |
| 6 fl oz single cream | |

Melt the butter without browning. Stir in the flour. Add $\frac{3}{4}$ pint of the chicken stock. Bring to the boil stirring all the time with a small balloon whisk (easier and more effective than a spoon).

Lower the heat and simmer for 5–6 minutes. Add the cream and sherry. Bring to the boil, then simmer for 15 minutes or so.

Strain into a clean pan. Add the mushrooms and continue simmering until they are cooked (about 6–7 minutes).

Fill the *vol-au-vent* with as many of the chicken pieces as will fill it: spoon over some of the delicate sauce. Garnish with two or three spears of asparagus.

Serve the remaining sauce, poured over the remaining chicken, separately along with the remaining asparagus spears. If you overfill the *vol-au-vent* it will go soggy. Cut the *vol-au-vent* into 4 or 6 serving portions, spooning extra chicken filling around the dish.

(*Note*: To come into line with modern cookery, this sauce is of a light consistency.) Serves 4–6

## Pears in Sauternes with Orange Rum Sabayon Sauce

8 even-sized ripe pears     Rind of 2 oranges
1 pt orange juice; fresh     2 oz castor sugar
  or bottled
1 pt Sauternes-type wine
  (I use Spanish)

Cut the orange rind into fine julienne strips. Bring the wine, orange juice and sugar to simmering point together with the orange rind.

Meanwhile using a potato peeler remove all the peel from the pears. Try to retain the stalk if possible as it is decorative. Poach the pears – lidded – until tender, which will take about 20 minutes. Remove them carefully to a serving dish. Strain the juice into a jug. Retain half a pint of this for the Sabayon Sauce.

Boil the remaining juice until syrupy together with the orange rind. Cool then spoon this syrup over the pears. Chill well.

*Sabayon Sauce (can be served hot or chilled)*
6 egg yolks     1 oz unsalted butter,
2 oz castor sugar      softened
½ pt cooking liquor
4 tbsp Jamaica Rum (or
  extra orange juice)

In a pyrex basin cream the yolks and sugar until light and fluffy. Whisk in – using a small balloon whisk – the liquor. Arrange the basin over a pan of boiling water and whisk steadily and consistently until the mixture thickens.

Using a cloth to protect the hands, remove the basin from the heat and immediately whisk in the rum (which will also reduce any residual heat which might curdle the sauce). Stand the bowl in a sink containing

2-3 inches of cold water, and continue whisking for a minute adding bits of the softened butter as you do this. When cool, cover with plastic wrap and chill.

Whisk again before serving.

# MENU 5

Gnocchi alla Romana
Poached Salmon with
Amontillado Sherry Cream Sauce
Petits Pots de Crème au Mocha

### Gnocchi alla Romana

If my memory serves me well, this was the very first dish I ever made when I was a student at Lausanne's famous hotel school.

Straight from Imperial Rome this economical dish ought to suit English palates well, as it is similar to a Batter, or Yorkshire, Pudding, though it is made with semolina. It is filling and tasty.

| | |
|---|---|
| $1\frac{3}{4}$ pt milk | 2 egg yolks |
| 7 oz semolina | $\frac{1}{2}$ tsp grated nutmeg |
| 4 oz freshly grated | Salt to taste |
|    Parmesan cheese | 3 oz butter |

Bring the milk, with 1 teaspoon of salt, to the boil, and lower the heat. 'Rain' in the semolina, stirring and beating all the time as you do this with a balloon whisk.

Cook this mixture over a low heat for 15 minutes until it becomes very thick. Take care it doesn't scorch.

Add half the grated cheese and 1 ounce of the butter, the nutmeg and the two yolks, beating each well in as you work. Dampen a work-surface and tip out the mixture onto it. Wet your right hand and press the mixture into a squarish shape, about $\frac{1}{2}$ inch thick.

Leave to cool completely (about 1½ hours).

Using a plain scone cutter or drinking glass 2 inches in diameter, cut the mixture into discs, dipping the implement into cold water between each cut. Butter an ovenproof dish. Cut the 'leavings' or débris of the mixture into inch bits, and lay them in the bottom of the dish. Dot with bits of the remaining butter and dredge with a little cheese.

Arrange the discs, overlapping somewhat, on top of this, dot each disc with butter and scatter over the rest of the cheese. Bake in a pre-heated oven at Gas Mark 8, 450°F for 15–20 minutes or until a good golden-brown crust has formed.

Serve with a tomato sauce (p. 46) (though they don't do this in Rome!) and a tossed salad. Serves 4–5 as a main dish.


## Poached Salmon with Amontillado Sherry Cream Sauce

| | |
|---|---|
| 4 × 1½ in. thick salmon cutlets (made from 2 × 10 oz salmon steaks) | ½ tsp salt |
| | 6 peppercorns |
| | Sprig dill or ¼ tsp dill herb, or sprig basil or |
| A knob of butter | tarragon |
| Dry white wine to cover | |

Choose a shallow pan which is just large enough to contain the salmon cutlets. Butter this.

Arrange the salmon in the pan. Pour over enough dry white wine to just cover. Add herbs and seasonings. Bring to the boil, reduce heat and simmer with a lid on (or cover with foil) for 10 minutes. Turn heat off and leave the fish for a further half-hour.

*Sherry Cream Sauce*

4 fl oz cooking stock
4 fl oz Amontillado
  sherry
12 fl oz double cream
A little salt

Freshly milled white
  pepper
1 tbsp freshly chopped
  basil, tarragon or dill

Reduce the stock, in which you have cooked the salmon cutlets, and sherry to 4 fluid ounces by boiling rapidly in an enamel or stainless steel pan.

Add the cream and reduce again to 10 fluid ounces ($\frac{1}{2}$ pint). Season delicately. Add the freshly chopped herbs just before serving.

If the cream shows signs of 'oiling', add a modicum of water and whisk this in. Serves 4


### Petits Pots de Crème au Mocha

2 tbsp strong liquid
  coffee or Nescafé
2 oz Bournville
  chocolate

$\frac{1}{2}$ pt single cream
2 egg yolks
$1\frac{1}{2}$ oz castor sugar

Break the chocolate into pieces and put into a small bowl with the coffee. Arrange the bowl over a pan of simmering water. When it has softened mix it together. In a non-stick pan, bring the cream to just boiling point, stirring from time to time. Mix in to the chocolate mixture away from the heat.

Cream the yolks and sugar together. Pour the hot mixture on to these whisking all the time.

Pour into ramekins. Stand these in a baking tray of hot water.

Bake at Gas Mark 4, 350°F for 20–25 minutes, or until set. Cool then chill well. Makes 4

# MENU 6

*Watercress Mousse*
*Navarin of Lamb*
*Red Fruit Brûlée*

**Watercress Mousse**

| | |
|---|---|
| 3 bunches watercress, washed and with fibres cut off | 1 sachet ($\frac{1}{2}$ oz) gelatine crystals |
| $\frac{1}{4}$ pt home-made mayonnaise | Dash of tabasco |
| $\frac{1}{4}$ pt double cream | 8 oz Ricotta or Philadelphia cream cheese |
| $\frac{1}{4}$ pt hot light chicken stock (use stock cube) | Salt and freshly milled pepper |

Beat the cheese until smooth. Mix in the mayonnaise. Melt the gelatine in the hot stock. Leave to cool.

With a food processor, make a purée of the watercress, including the stalks, using the cooled gelatine as liquid. Add tabasco and seasoning.

Whip the cream until it *just* holds soft peaks. Cut and mix this into the mayonnaise/cheese mixture, then cut and mix the purée into this.

Pour into individual ramekins (6 to 8, depending on their size), or $1 \times 1\frac{1}{2}$ pint dish or mould. Chill. Eat with a teaspoon. Serves 6–8

### Navarin of Lamb

2½ lb leg of lamb (cheaper cuts can be used for family cooking)

1 tbsp seasoned flour (see method)

8 oz carrots cut into sticks

8 oz celery cut into ¼ in. dice

2 cloves garlic, crushed

4 oz tomato purée

Large sprig thyme (or level tsp dried)

Small sprig rosemary (or ¼ tsp dried)

½ oz flour

Salt and freshly milled pepper

1 tsp paprika

¼ pt stock (use stock cube)

½ pt dry white wine

1 dozen baby onions par-boiled (pickling onions will do)

1 oz lard

1 dsp castor sugar

4 large tomatoes, de-seeded and chopped

Oil for frying

1 heaped tbsp freshly chopped tarragon or parsley

Completely strip the meat of any skin and as much of the fat as you like. Cut into inch-square cubes, toss in a tablespoon of flour seasoned with salt, black pepper and a teaspoon paprika. (Shake the meat and flour in a large polythene bag for this operation.)

Heat 1 tablespoon of oil in a heavy-bottomed frying pan. Fry the cubes of meat until brown, moving them about to colour them evenly. Do this in three batches, putting each batch into an earthenware casserole when finished. Now add the tomato purée and mix well. Sprinkle over the ½ ounce of flour and stir in. Add the garlic, rosemary and thyme. Season.

Back to the frying pan: in a further tablespoon of oil, lightly brown the carrots and celery and add them to the casserole. Cover with the stock and wine and cook gently until the meat is tender. This will take about 1½ hours in a pre-heated oven Gas Mark 5, 375°F.

Meanwhile melt the lard in a frying pan, add the sugar, put in the par-boiled onions and toss them around over a good heat until nicely caramelised. Remove with a draining spoon and keep them warm for garnishing.

When the lamb is tender skim off any surplus fats. Add the chopped tomatoes and return the casserole to the oven for five minutes to heat these through. Just before serving scatter the onions over the top and sprinkle liberally with freshly chopped tarragon or parsley. Serves 4

### Red Fruit *Brûlée*

| | |
|---|---|
| 8 oz punnet redcurrants | 2 oz (or less) castor sugar |
| 8 oz fresh raspberries | 4 egg yolks |
| 8 oz strawberries, cut into quarters | 2 whole eggs |
| | 1 tsp cornflour |
| 2 tbsp liqueur (such as orange Curaçao, Grand Marnier, Drambuie) | Vanilla pod or 1 tsp vanilla essence |
| 1 tbsp castor sugar | Enough castor sugar for the topping |
| 1 pt single cream | |

Clean the fruit, splash with the liqueur, dredge with 1 tablespoon of sugar, cover with plastic film and chill for two hours or more.

Meanwhile, cream the eggs, yolks, 2 ounces of sugar and cornflour in a heatproof bowl. Bring the cream to the boil having added the vanilla to it and pour over the egg mixture whisking well all the time. The cream should thicken, but this depends on many factors, so if it doesn't, arrange the bowl over a pan of boiling water and whisk steadily but thoroughly until it does. Stand the bowl immediately in a sink of cold water and continue whisking until the residual heat has gone.

Leave to cool completely. Chill well.

Put the chilled fruits in the bottom of a 3 inch deep 2 to 2½ pint flameproof dish. Pour the thickened cream over this. Dredge the top completely with enough castor sugar to give about an eighth of an inch layer. Stand the dish in a second tin or dish containing ice-cold water. Brown under a pre-heated spanking hot grill. Leave to cool. Serve cold. (Do not refrigerate because if you do the topping will soften.) Serves 6–8

# MENU 7

*Buttered Eggs in a Shell*
*Glazed Loin of Pork*
*Braised Red Cabbage*
*Chocolate Gooseberry Cake*

**Buttered Eggs in a Shell**

This novelty for Easter Day brunch or as a starter at a dinner party is a good enough reason to use that antique egg cruet!

4 eggs
⅛ pt single cream, or top of milk
1½ oz butter

Salt and milled white pepper
Pinch nutmeg or ground coriander

*Garnish (optional and variable to taste)*
1 small jar caviar or lumpfish roe
1 tomato, skinned, de-seeded and cut into small dice

4 small mushrooms, chopped, seasoned and quickly sautéed in a knob of butter

Have any garnish used at the ready.

Using a small fine saw-edged knife or steel nail file very gently saw off the top of each egg at the pointed end and about quarter of the way down. To do this rest the egg on a crumpled towel and don't apply any pressure with the knife or finger. Don't attempt to saw right through until you have sawn a groove right round. This way you'll get a clean break. Pour out the egg yolks and whites.

Beat the eggs well, season and add a smidge of nutmeg or ground coriander.

Stir in the cream.

Melt an ounce of the butter in a small pan, then over a *low* heat, 'draw' the egg mixture in the pan until it is beginning to set.

Squeeze or spoon the remaining butter over the mixture, fill into the egg shells, garnish appropriately and serve.


**Glazed Loin of Pork**

There are certain food (and wine) marriages which seem unbreakable, like our national Roast Beef and Yorkshire Pudding, Boiled Ham with Broad Beans and Parsley Sauce, Roast Capon with Bread Sauce and so on.

And no matter how many new ideas we think up 'for a change', the old familiar pairing always fits our appetite like a favourite jacket if you'll forgive the attempt at a simile.

For this recipe I have looked abroad to foreign shores for a marriage which could well enjoy a honeymoon here.

The Scandinavians, Germans and Austrians all enjoy Roast Pork with Red Cabbage. We tend to under-estimate the value of this vegetable which grows abundantly here and is cheap (thus releasing some house-keeping pennies to make it into a succulent mouth-watering Sunday lunch treat!). The secret – if secret there is – is to shred the cabbage as finely as possible.

| Piece of loin of pork | 1 level tsp freshly |
|---|---|
| allowing 1 'bone' per | milled black pepper* |
| serving (approx. | 1 level tsp mustard* |
| 3–4 lb) for 6 people | 1 tsp white flour |
| 1 oz butter* | $\frac{1}{2}$ chicken stock cube |
| 1 level tsp salt* | $\frac{1}{2}$ pt red wine |

Have your butcher chine the loin and score the skin diagonally across both ways. (You can do this yourself with a Stanley knife.) Make a paste with the asterisked ingredients and rub all over the skin.

Stand the loin on a rack in a roasting tin. Roast at Gas Mark 6, 400°F for 1 hour.

Remove from the oven and take off the crackling (this may or may not come off in one piece – it doesn't matter as you will want to break it into pieces for serving).

Have ready the following glaze:

| 1 tbsp thick honey | 1 tbsp soy sauce |
|---|---|
| 1 tsp grated orange rind | 1 clove garlic, crushed |
| 1 heaped tsp dry mustard | (optional) |
| 1 tsp salt | |

Mix all these ingredients into a paste. Re-score the *fat* on the loin so that the glaze seeps into it. Spread the glaze over. Turn the oven up to Gas Mark 8, 450°F.

Drain away all but 1 tablespoon of the fats in the roasting tin. Sprinkle over 1 teaspoon white flour and work well in. Crumble in half a chicken stock cube. Pour in $\frac{1}{2}$ pint red wine. Stand the loin in all this and return to the hot oven for half an hour or until glazed.

Remove the loin to a warm serving dish. Strain the 'gravy' into a pan. Let it stand for 5 minutes. Skim off any excess fats. Then bring to the boil and boil rapidly until reduced by about one-third.

Carve the loin, or cut into chops. Spoon over a little of the rich red wine sauce.

Serve with the red cabbage (see p. 59) and a mealy jacket potato with plenty of good butter or soured cream and some freshly chopped chives. Serves 6

## Chocolate and Gooseberry Cake

If you don't have gooseberry jam, then any jam with a sharp-edged taste will do, such as raspberry, redcurrant (Krakus do a very tangy redcurrant jam which I commend to you).

8 oz unsalted butter at room temperature
4 oz castor sugar
4 large eggs
6 oz self-raising flour, 2 oz cocoa powder, sifted together with 1 tsp baking powder

2 oz ground almonds, sieved (*or* an extra 2 oz of flour)
1 tsp vanilla essence
Gooseberry jam
2–3 tbsp milk or water

*Chocolate Butter Cream*
4 oz unsalted butter, softened
4 oz (or less) icing sugar

2 oz cocoa powder
1 tsp vanilla essence

*Chocolate Icing*
4 oz dark chocolate
1 oz unsalted butter

1 tbsp brandy or whisky

*Chocolate Leaves*
8 oz bar of chocolate

Butter and line two 8 inch sandwich tins.

Cream the butter and sugar thoroughly. Beat the

eggs and add to the creamed mixture gradually, adding the essence and a little of the flour mixture if it shows signs of curdling. Fold the sifted flour, cocoa and baking powder in thoroughly, adding the modest amount of ground almonds as you go along. Add 2 to 3 tablespoons of milk or water, or enough to arrive at a loose dropping consistency.

Divide equally between the two tins, and bake in a moderate oven at Gas Mark 5, 375°F for 35–40 minutes. Leave for 5 minutes before turning onto a wire cooling tray. Remove the paper.

Make up the butter cream by blending all the ingredients together to a smooth paste.

To make the icing, break the chocolate into bits and soften, together with the butter and brandy or whisky in a basin over a pan of simmering water. Leave to cool before spreading over the top of the cake.

To make up the cake, spread a good cushion of gooseberry jam over the bottom cake. Spread over the butter cream. Invert the top cake so that it is flat side up.

Spread the icing over the top (this is a softish icing). Decorate at will with chocolate leaves made up as follows. Melt the bar of chocolate in a bowl over simmering water. Select even-sized bay or rose leaves, or small camellia leaves. Brush melted chocolate over the front of the leaves, put to set in the fridge until hard. Peel off the leaves carefully.

An alternative way to assemble this rich cake would be to split the two sandwich cakes in half, spread the first layer with jam, the second with all the butter cream, then a third with jam again before putting on the top and icing it.

*Note*: All cake tins, whether regular or non-stick, should be buttered and lined at the bottom with buttered paper.

# MENU 8

Avocado Salad with Foie Gras and Tarragon
Broccoli and Lobster Flan
Norwegian Cream

## Avocado Salad with *Foie Gras* and Tarragon

1 tin *Bloc de Foie Gras
  de Canard au Poivre
  Vert* (5–6 oz)
4 large ripe avocados

Lemon juice
6 artichoke hearts
  (tinned will do)
1 × 8 oz tin hearts of palm

*Dressing*
⅛ pt rich olive oil
1 tsp tarragon mustard
Juice of half lemon
Salt and milled pepper

Good pinch castor sugar
1 tbsp freshly chopped
  tarragon

Place the tin of *foie gras* into the fridge overnight to set. (*Swiss Parfait* can be used for a poor man's version of this salad.)

Put all the ingredients for the dressing into a screw-topped jar and shake until everything is emulsified.

Cut the avocados in half and brush well with lemon juice. If you prepare them earlier in the day for the evening meal pour the lemon juice into a shallow glass or china dish and stand the avocados, flesh down, in this until ready for use.

Quarter the artichoke hearts. Drain, rinse and drain again the hearts of palm. Cut into cubes, discarding any which are 'woody'.

39

Open both ends of the *foie gras* tin and push the pâté out.

Using a knife dipped into boiling water, cut the chilled *foie gras* into cubes. Mix the cubed ingredients together. Carefully place the cubes into the avocado and cover with the dressing.

**Broccoli and Lobster Flan**

Line a 1½ inch deep 8–9 inch diameter flan ring with pastry made from:

| | |
|---|---|
| 6 oz plain white flour | 1 level tsp salt |
| 2 oz butter | 1 egg yolk beaten with |
| 2 oz lard | 3 tbsp ice-cold water |

*Filling*

| | |
|---|---|
| 12 fl oz single cream | 12 oz broccoli |
| 4 large eggs, beaten | Chicken stock (from |
| Salt and freshly milled | stock cube) |
| pepper, plus good | Juice of half a lemon |
| pinch of mace | |
| 3 lobster tails or | |
| 12 oz crayfish or | |
| jumbo prawns | |

Bake the flan case blind at Gas Mark 6, 400°F for 20 minutes.

Break the broccoli into tiny florets, and poach for 1 minute in chicken stock, well acidulated with lemon. Drain and cool.

Slice the lobster tails into manageable pieces.

Season the beaten eggs. Bring the cream to the boil and pour over the eggs, whisking well as you do this. Arrange the lobster tails attractively in the base of the flan. Disperse the broccoli florets in and amongst them. Pour the savoury custard over this.

Bake at Gas Mark 3, 325°F for 35–40 minutes, or until the custard is set. Serve either hot, warm or cold. Serves 8

## Norwegian Cream

This custard-cum-trifle is one of my favourite sweets. I have played around with this recipe over the years, and this below is how it stands to date. It is much improved on the original and is ideal for transporting on a picnic in its own glass or china bowl, or as part of a dinner or buffet menu.

1 pt single cream
2 tsp vanilla essence
1 oz (or more) castor sugar
1 tsp finely grated orange rind
4 large eggs
1 × 12 oz tin apricot caps or a dozen fresh apricots pitted and halved
Half jar apricot jam

Juice of half an orange
3 tbsp Cointreau or Grand Marnier (2 miniature bottles)
3 slices white bread, de-crusted and made into rough crumbs
1 oz unsalted butter for frying
½ pt whipped cream (optional)
Few glacé apricots (optional)

Melt the butter in a heavy-bottomed frying pan. Add the bread crumbs and, stirring all the time, let them acquire a good golden colour and become quite crisp. Splash 1 teaspoon of vanilla essence over the crumbs during the frying process. Leave to cool completely.

Meanwhile, bring the single cream, together with the second teaspoon of vanilla essence and the grated orange rind, slowly to the boil so that all infuses. Beat the eggs with the sugar in a bowl. Pour the boiling cream over this, whisking all the time.

Mix the orange juice with the jam and spread onto the bottom of an ovenproof dish, about 3 to 4 inches deep.

Distribute the drained apricot caps evenly over the jam.

Add the liqueur to the custard mixture and pour into the dish. Stand the dish in a second one containing hot water.

Bake at Gas Mark 4, 350°F for 30–40 minutes or until the custard is just set.

Leave to cool completely.

Spread the cold crisp crumbs over the top. Pipe round a collar of whipped cream and decorate with extra glacé apricots if you are feeling in a lavish mood – for this you will require an extra ½ pint whipped cream and some glacé apricots. Serves 8

# MENU 9

Minestrone
Stuffed Boned Capon
Tomato Madeira Sauce
Gooseberry Fool with Rose-flower Water

## Minestrone

There are as many 'right' ways of making this soup as there are for making fruit cake; it is the type of soup that cannot really go wrong, though I prefer to control just when certain items go into the pot in an attempt to retain a bit of their character. I cook the pasta separately, for example, and I don't add the green vegetables until just before everything is cooked in order to retain their pretty green colour: but it doesn't matter a hoot really. I think it has to be made for a lot of people or for a large family and it keeps and re-heats well.

I don't think it is necessary for you to put in everything, but try to get as many of the items together as you can. My recipe is fulsome, perhaps too fulsome for some, in which case just add a little more stock or water.

The only essential ingredient is the freshly grated Parmesan cheese, but this may be difficult to obtain in your particular area, so bottled or tinned will have to do, but this does tend to be a bit grainy.

Why not buy Parmesan by post? It keeps almost for ever!

6 oz pasta 'bows' or spaghetti broken into 2 in. pieces and cooked separately
3 tbsp olive oil
4 rashers unsmoked bacon cut into striplets
1 large onion, chopped
½ head celery, chopped
2 cloves garlic, crushed
2 tbsp tomato purée
4 pt chicken stock
4 carrots cut into discs
1 small cauliflower broken into tiny florets
8 oz tin flageolet beans (or haricot beans soaked overnight in boiling water), drained and rinsed
4 oz salami, cut into strips
Salt and freshly milled pepper
Small packet *petits pois*
Small packet cut French beans
4 tomatoes, de-seeded and chopped
2 tbsp freshly chopped parsley (or basil as it adds a lovely flavour)
Water (see method)

*Garnish*
Freshly grated
    Parmesan cheese

Cook the pasta separately in boiling lightly salted water for 15 minutes. Drain and reserve.

Heat the oil in a large (8–10 pint) heavy-bottomed pan. Fry the bacon until golden-brown. Add the onion and celery and fry this for 10 minutes over a low heat until it is transparent and golden.

Add the garlic and tomato purée and continue frying for a further 5 minutes, stirring to ensure that nothing burns.

Pour in the stock and bring to the boil. Add the carrots, and after 10 minutes add the cauliflower florets, flageolets and salami. Simmer for a further 15 to 20 minutes.

Season lightly with salt and milled pepper.

Add the cooked pasta, peas, French beans and chopped tomatoes and cook at a steady roll for a further 15 minutes or so.

If you prefer your Minestrone less thick, add half a pint or more of water or stock just before adding the pasta. Sprinkle in the chopped parsley just before you ladle the soup into warm (preferably) earthenware bowls.

Pass round grated Parmesan cheese for people to help themselves, and chunks of garlic bread for dunking. Serves 8 good family helpings.


## Stuffed Boned Capon

The capon can be prepared a day in advance.

6–7 lb capon (boned)

### Ham and Brazil Nut Stuffing

| | |
|---|---|
| 1 lb piece of gammon, ham soaked overnight in cold water | 4 oz brazil nuts, roughly chopped |
| 1 oz butter | 1 tsp tomato purée |
| 1 small onion, finely chopped | 1 tsp finely grated orange zest |
| 4 oz fresh white breadcrumbs | 1 egg, beaten |

$\frac{1}{2}$ tsp ground mace          4 oz soft butter
Salt and milled pepper

### Stuffing

Cut gammon into small pieces and fry in 1 ounce butter for 2–3 minutes only. Turn the ham, but let it take on a little colour. Remove the ham pieces with a slotted spoon. Soften onion in the juices until transparent.

Put the ham and onion through the fine blade of a mincer. Mix with the rest of the ingredients and bind with the egg. No salt will be needed.

Form the stuffing into an oval shape. Turn the boned capon skin-side down on to a work surface. Spread it out whichever way it wants to go.

Place the stuffing on top of the breast section. Then wrap, fold and tuck the leg and wing meat (and skin) round this, arriving at a nice shape.

Thread a bodkin with fine string or linen thread and approach the next step as if you were darning a badly torn and worn quilted dressing-gown, darning, tucking and holding the seams together to hold in any stuffing or flesh. Sew and bind up.

Spread 4 oz butter over the surface, seasoning with salt and pepper and $\frac{1}{2}$ teaspoon of ground mace.

Stand the capon on a rack in a roasting tin. Cover with foil. Roast at Gas Mark 6, 400°F for 2 hours, lowering the temperature to Gas Mark 4, 350°F after an hour.

Serve cut into handsome $\frac{1}{2}$ inch thick slices. Pour a ladle of Tomato Madeira Sauce (see below) round each slice. Serves 6–8

**Tomato Madeira Sauce**

Whilst this is a modest amount of sauce, it is easier to use a large 5–6 pint pan.

1 oz butter or olive oil
  for frying
1 medium (3 oz) onion,
  chopped
1 medium (3 oz) carrot,
  cut into small dice
1 oz mushrooms, cut into
  dice

1 heaped dsp tomato
  purée
1 heaped tsp (approx.
  half an ounce) flour
1 level tsp mild paprika
$\frac{1}{4}$ pt red wine
$\frac{1}{4}$ pt dry Madeira

1 pt strong chicken stock (made from capon bones or use 1½ stock cubes)
Extra small glass dry or medium dry Madeira
½ lb fresh tomatoes, skinned, de-seeded and roughly chopped
Salt if needed

Melt the butter letting it take on an almond flavour and golden colour.

Add the onion and carrot. Lower heat and brown, stirring regularly.

Add the mushrooms and mix in the purée, letting it take on a little colour – but it must not burn. Sprinkle over the flour, add paprika, stir in well and allow to colour for a minute, stirring all the time.

Turn the fried mixture onto a dinner plate. Turn up the heat and pour in the red wine. Work all the residues from the bottom of the pan into the wine.

Add the Madeira, stock, tomatoes and the fried vegetable mixture. Bring everything to the boil. Reduce the heat, simmer the sauce for 30 minutes, when you will have approximately 1 pint of sauce. Strain into a clean pan through a fine-meshed strainer. Leave to cool. Refrigerate until needed. (This sauce can be made two days in advance.)

To serve: bring the sauce to the boil. Add a small glass of dry or medium dry Madeira, strain again into a sauce-boat and serve.

The sauce can be further enriched by whisking in 1 ounce of fridge-hard French or Dutch butter cut into cubes immediately – after re-heating, but before pouring into the bowl. Once the butter is whisked in, the sauce should not be boiled. Serves 6–8

# Gooseberry Fool with Rose-flower Water

The gooseberry is essentially an English fruit and peculiar to us. In pies, jam, tarts and puddings it shows its acid tartness well.

Small green gooseberries have the best flavour and are ideal for that most English of puds – the Fool.

1 lb young green gooseberries
2 oz unsalted butter
4 oz (or less) sugar

$\frac{1}{2}$ pt double cream
1 tbsp triple-strength rose-flower water

Top, tail and wash the gooseberries. Melt the butter without letting it take any colour. Add the gooseberries, put on a lid and cook for 10 minutes or until soft, over a low heat. Remove the pan from the heat and sweeten to taste. Add the rose-flower water and mix in. Leave to cool.

Put the fruit through the fine grid of a mouli (a blender makes the purée too foamy). Whip the cream until it stands in soft peaks. Fold into the cooled purée. Spoon into individual glasses. Chill, covered with cling film. Serves 6

# MENU 10

*Eggs with Avocado
and Watercress Mayonnaise
Old English Duck Pie with
Forcemeat Balls and Chestnuts
Fig 'Sue'*

## Eggs with Avocado and Watercress Mayonnaise

Served with eggs, this sauce gives a new dimension to that ubiquitous starter, the egg mayonnaise. The sauce is also excellent with cold poached salmon or chicken.

6 oz home-made
  mayonnaise
3 Hass avocados (or 2
  larger ones), peeled
  and pitted
2 bunches of virile
  watercress, picked
1 bunch chives, roughly
  chopped
2 good sprigs of fresh
  basil if available
Juice of 1 lemon
Salt and milled pepper
6 hard-boiled eggs

With a food processor blend all the ingredients together. If you wish, you can press through a fine sieve for extra refinement. If the sauce is too stiff (it should have a consistency of heavy pouring cream) thin it down with a little cold water.

## Old English Duck Pie with Forcemeat Balls and Chestnuts

1 × 12 oz packet flaky pastry, or 12 oz home-made rough puff or shortcrust pastry
1 × 4 lb duck
1 onion, chopped
1 clove garlic, crushed
8 oz oyster or field mushrooms, quartered
1 oz tin of chestnuts in brine or fresh roasted chestnuts
8 oz unsmoked bacon, cut into sticks

1 orange zest and juice
½ bottle red wine
1 tsp flour
½ tin plus, duck or game consommé
1 sprig or 1 tsp dried sage
1 sprig or 1 tsp dried thyme
Salt and pepper
Oil for frying

*Forcemeat Balls*
6 oz lean pork or veal, cut up
4 oz pork fat, cut up
1 duck's liver, diced
1 level tsp nutmeg

2 tbsp medium sherry
1 egg, beaten
2 tsp salt
Oil for frying

First make the forcemeat balls by putting the pork and fat twice through the fine blade of a mincer.

Mix in the rest of the ingredients. (This can be done with a food processor, mixing in the duck liver last to retain texture.)

Form into 12–14 small flattish balls or 'cakes'. Brown quickly in a little smoking oil. Set aside.

Have your poulterer cut the duck into eight pieces, removing excess carcass bones and using these for stock or soup.

In a very little smoking oil, well-brown the duck pieces a few at a time. Transfer to an ovenproof pot. Sprinkle the flour over the duck pieces.

In the pan oils, brown the bacon sticks, onion and mushrooms. Add to the pot using a draining spoon. Add the orange rind and juice, red wine and enough consommé to *just* cover. Add salt and pepper and the herbs and garlic. Put lid on. Cook at Gas Mark 6, 400°F for 45 minutes.

Meanwhile, roll out the pastry. Cut a lid to cover a pie dish (approx. 10 × 7 × 4). Cut off strips to rim the dish, and cut out any decorations such as circles, leaves, etc.

Transfer the contents of the oven-proof pot to the pie dish. Disperse the forcemeat balls in and amongst the duck. Fit the pastry lid in the usual way, adding any decorations. Brush with a little egg or milk and bake at Gas Mark 8, 450°F for 15 minutes, then Gas Mark 4, 350°F for a further 45 minutes. (For those who don't like the rich duck skin, this can be taken off after the first cooking, before the pieces are put into the pie dish.) Serves 5–6

### Fig 'Sue'

I have based this dish on a regional dish from Cumbria.

12 oz dried figs
$\frac{1}{2}$ pt dark ale (Bass Barley Wine)
4 oz Demerara sugar (or less)

$\frac{1}{4}$ pt double cream, whipped
1 tsp grated orange rind
2 tbsp Demerara rum

Cut the figs in half. Put into a bowl. Bring the ale to boiling point, pour over the figs adding enough hot water just to cover if necessary. Leave overnight.

Next day simmer until tender with the sugar and orange rind. Strain and blend to a fine purée. Rub through a hair sieve, using some of the cooking syrup. Cool. Stir in the rum and whipped cream. Spoon into glasses. Chill well. Serves 4–6

# MENU 11

*Chilled Cream of Tomato Soup
with Turmeric, Orange and Shrimps
Cold Pâté Stuffed Duck
Orange Soufflé (Hot)*

**Chilled Cream of Tomato Soup with Turmeric, Orange and Shrimps**

This soup is perhaps best when served very well chilled and in smallish portions as it is very rich: it can be served hot, in which case do not put in the shrimps until it is ready for serving or they will toughen.

14 fl oz tomato juice
1 level tsp turmeric
1 level tsp mild curry
   powder
2 cloves garlic, crushed

½ pt double cream
1 tsp castor sugar
Juice of half a lemon
1 heaped tsp finely
   grated orange rind

*Garnish*
2 navel oranges,
   segmented
2 tomatoes, skinned,
   de-seeded and cut into
   dice

4 oz peeled shrimps
   (frozen or fresh)

Put all the ingredients except the cream into a heavy-bottomed pan, bring to the boil and simmer for 10 minutes. Add the cream and simmer for a further 10 minutes.

Leave to cool. Strain into a bowl, cover with cling-film and chill well, preferably overnight.

Ladle into chilled soup cups, and garnish each with a little of the diced tomato, two or three orange segments and some shrimps. Serves 4–5

## Cold Pâté Stuffed Duck

This rich way of preparing cold duck is popular in Denmark where I originally came across it many moons ago. It forms part of their famous *koldbord* or cold table. I suggest you serve it as a first course, together with slivers of Brasola, smoked loin of pork, smoked goose, or Parma ham. Even silverside or pastrami could be part of the medley for a buffet or elaborate first course.

1 cold roast duck
    (4–5 lb)

*Filling*

| | |
|---|---|
| 1 × 12 oz tin Swiss Parfait | Level tsp black pepper |
| 6 oz unsalted butter | Squeeze lemon juice |
| Level tsp nutmeg | 3 tbsp whisky or rum |

Make a fine purée from all the filling ingredients using a blender.

Cut the breasts off the duck by cutting down either side of the breast bone, following the wishbone round. Carefully lift each breast away, cutting where it adheres to the carcass. Lay the breasts side by side on a cutting-board and, holding the knife at an angle of 45°, cut diagonal pieces half an inch thick. You should get 7 to 8 slices from each side.

Fill a piping bag fitted with a rose tube with half of the pâté mixture. Spread the remaining pâté on the bared breast bones. Using a palette knife, carefully lift each cut breast and lay it back where it came from!

Pipe a column of rich pâté down the centre of the breasts, dispersing any left over at will. Serves 8 as a starter with other meats, or 4 on its own.


### Orange Soufflé (Hot)

| | |
|---|---|
| 2 oranges | 1 oz unsalted butter |
| 4 tbsp orange Curaçao or whisky | 3 oz castor sugar |
| | $2\frac{1}{2}$ oz plain flour |
| 3 oz dryish sponge cake crumbs (use trifle biscuits if necessary) | 4 egg yolks |
| | 5 egg whites |
| | Extra icing sugar |
| $\frac{1}{2}$ pt milk | |

Carefully butter a 3 pint soufflé dish with unsalted butter. Finely grate the zest from the oranges. Put in a bowl with 1 tablespoon of the liqueur. Knife-peel the oranges and segment them. Set these aside. In a basin soak the crumbs in a further tablespoon of the liqueur. Add the segments. In a bowl make a paste with a little of the milk, sugar and the flour. Bring the rest of the milk to the boil together with the butter. Slowly incorporate this into the flour mixture, using a balloon whisk to facilitate this.

Cook the mixture over a low heat until it leaves the sides of the pan (it will be stiffish). Remove the pan from the heat and whisk in the remaining Curaçao or whisky and zest. Beat or whisk in the yolks one by one.

Whip the egg whites until they stand in stiff peaks.

Mix one-third of these well into the mixture, then lightly cut and fold in the remaining whites. Pour half the mixture into the soufflé dish. Spoon over the crumbs and segments, then the remaining half of the soufflé mixture. Level the top.

Bake in a pre-heated oven on a pre-heated baking sheet at Gas Mark 6, 400°F for 45 minutes.

Dust with icing sugar and serve immediately. Serves 5–6

# MENU 12

*Chilled Pea, Mint and Lemon Soup*
*with Soured Cream*
*Beef and Red Pepper Sauce*
*(to serve with pasta)*
*Apple Butter Creams*

**Chilled Pea, Mint and Lemon Soup with Soured Cream**

| | |
|---|---|
| 1 lb packet tiny frozen peas | 1 pt cold chicken stock (use stock cube) |
| 2 tsp sugar | Juice and rind of 1 lemon |
| 1 clove garlic, crushed | $\frac{1}{2}$ pt single cream |
| 1 large bunch of mint, picked | $\frac{1}{4}$ pt carton soured cream |

Toss the peas for 5–6 minutes with the sugar and crushed garlic and mint in a pan over a low heat, using *no* liquid.

When the juices are fully drawn and the peas tender, leave them to cool. Add the lemon juice and 1 teaspoon of the zest. Put through a food mill (a blender makes the soup too smooth, though this is a fine detail).

Stir in the single cream, then add enough chicken stock to make a soup of the consistency of single cream.

Chill well – for example, leave overnight in a fridge.

Serve each portion with a spoonful of soured cream for guests to stir in at will. Extra mint can be passed, but it has to be remembered that chopped mint does discolour, so you may choose not to do this and serve snipped chives instead. Serves 5–6

**Beef and Red Pepper Sauce** (to serve with pasta)

For Bolognese addicts this will be a winner. I have omitted flour – well, almost – and used a purée of peppers to cohere the whole thing. Good for dieters too. Serve it with any pasta, adding extra peppers cut into julienne strips if liked. These should be softened in a little olive oil or butter before mixing in with the pasta.

| | |
|---|---|
| 1 lb best steak, fat and sinew free, minced | 1 × 2 oz tin anchovy fillets |
| 4 tbsp olive oil | 1 tsp flour |
| 1 medium onion, finely chopped | 3 red peppers |
| | 2 dashes tabasco sauce |
| 1 × 4 oz tin tomato purée | 1 tsp brown sugar |
| Half a bottle of red wine | Salt and pepper |
| 1 tsp paprika | |

Heat 2 tablespoons of the oil in a fire-proof pot. Soften the onion, then add the mince a little at a time letting it take what colour it will.

Mix in the flour, the paprika and the anchovy fillets. Pour the red wine over this. Cook at Gas Mark 6, 400°F for half an hour.

Meanwhile, de-seed the three red peppers, chop roughly, and over a low heat soften them *completely* in 2 tablespoons of oil, adding a teaspoon of brown sugar and a couple of dashes of tabasco.

In a blender or food processor, make the peppers into a fine purée. Stir this into the cooking meat sauce and cook for a further half-hour. Freezes well. Serves 8–10

## Apple Butter Creams

1 lb dessert apples
Sugar to taste (2–4 oz)
Grated rind and juice of
  1 large orange
4 oz unsalted butter,
  softened

1 tbsp orange flower
  water
3 tbsp dry white wine
$\frac{1}{2}$ pt double cream,
  whipped to soft peak

Wash, quarter and core the apples – do not peel. Put into a pan with the juice and rind and white wine.

Over a low heat (as you don't have a lot of liquid) toss and cook the apples until fully pulped. Stir in the sugar and flower water. Blend to a fine purée allowing the fruit to cool down to warm. Blend in the softened butter at a temperature that will not melt it or it will go grainy – edible but not so smooth to the palate. Cut and fold in the cream. Spoon into a bowl or glasses. Chill well. Serves 5–6

# A Selection of Vegetables and Salads

These can be served with or alongside your chosen main course. Some of the salads can also be served in smaller portions as starters, or in larger portions for a light lunch main dish.

## Braised Red Cabbage

2 oz butter
2 lb finely shredded red cabbage weighed after trimming and shredding
1 large onion, finely sliced
2 Cox's apples (cored but not peeled), grated
8 oz Muscatel or other seedless raisins

1 level tsp cornflour
2 × 2 in. strips orange rind (taken off with a potato peeler)
Juice of one orange
½ pt Red Burgundy-type wine
Level tsp milled black pepper
1 tsp salt

Melt the butter in a large pan or casserole of a size to fit your oven.

Add the onion. Lower the heat, put on a lid and soften the onion without letting it get more than a pale golden colour (for about 4 minutes).

Add the cabbage and toss and stir this until all is well mixed in. Sprinkle over the modicum of corn-flour, and mix in.

Add all the rest of the ingredients, including the wine. Bring to the boil. Put a lid on and transfer the casserole to a pre-heated oven, Gas Mark 5, 375°F for 1 to 1½ hours or until the cabbage is tender and the contents somewhat cohered. Serves 5–6

The cabbage is improved if it is made the day before and then reheated at Gas Mark 6, 400°F.

## Courgettes with Peas and Herbs

8 oz packet frozen *petits pois* (de-frosted)
4 medium-sized (5 in.) courgettes
Juice of half a lemon
1 oz butter
1 level tsp castor sugar
1 tbsp freshly-chopped herbs (basil or oregano in the summer). $1\frac{1}{2}$ tsp dried oregano in the winter
Salt and milled pepper

Top, tail and wash the courgettes. Cut into $\frac{1}{4}$ inch cubes. Toss in the lemon juice to prevent discoloration.

In a shallow, heavy-bottomed pan, melt the butter without browning. Add the peas and courgettes and all the remaining ingredients. Using a slotted spoon, turn and stir gently all the time, until everything is piping hot. The courgettes should still be somewhat crisp. Turn into a warm tureen and serve in the juices emitted. Serves 4

## Cream Cheese Stuffed Potatoes

3 medium even-sized potatoes
6 oz full fat cream cheese
1 oz butter, softened
Half a bunch of spring onions, chopped
Salt and pepper

Bake the potatoes in their jackets in the usual way, having rubbed the skins with butter (or oil or bacon fat) to make them crisp.

Cream the cheese and butter. Cut the potatoes in half, scoop out the flesh, push through a ricer or mash well. (Do *not* use a food processor as this will glutinise them!)

Beat in the cheese mixture and half the spring onions. Season well. Pile into the empty potato shells. Re-heat in the oven for 15 minutes or so at Gas Mark 6, 400°F. (These can be made in advance.) Sprinkle with the remaining spring onions. Serve piping hot.
Serves 6


### Cauliflower and Broccoli Vinaigrette (hot)

Vinaigrette dressing is not to be restricted to cold foods. It makes an admirable dressing for hot vegetables.

| | |
|---|---|
| 1 medium cauliflower cut into 8 pieces | 4 good broccoli heads cut into 8 pieces |

In a pan of boiling, salted water, cook the cauliflower for 5–6 minutes if you prefer it crisp, longer if you like vegetables well cooked.

Drain well and keep warm in a lidded tureen.

Cook the broccoli in the same water for the same length of time. Drain and arrange in and amongst the cauliflower.

Pour the following dressing over the cauliflower and broccoli.

| | |
|---|---|
| 6 tbsp olive or arachide oil (or a mixture of both)* | 2 tsp castor sugar* |
| | 1 bunch chives, finely chopped |
| 3 tbsp lemon juice* | 2 tbsp parsley, finely chopped |
| Level tsp salt* | |
| Level tsp dry mustard* | |
| Level tsp milled black pepper* | |

Shake the asterisked ingredients in a screw-topped jar until well emulsified. Then stir in the fresh herbs (any herbs will do: basil is also an excellent herb with cauliflower, as is mint.) Serves 4–5

## Snow Peas with Lemon and Orange

¾ lb snow peas
  (*mange-tout*)
Salted water
1½ oz unsalted butter
Zest of 1 small orange

Zest of ½ small lemon
1 tbsp lemon juice
1 tsp castor sugar
Pinch of salt

Bring a large pan of lightly salted water to the boil. Throw in the peas and boil rapidly for 3 minutes. Drain well. Return to the hot pan. Put lid on.

Have the butter ready, melted, to which you have added the lemon juice and the two rinds, a pinch of salt and the sugar.

Pour this hot mixture over the hot peas. Toss well and serve. Serves 4

## Purée of French Beans

1 lb French beans,
  topped, tailed and
  stringed
2 fl oz double cream

1 oz unsalted butter
Salt and freshly milled
  white pepper

Boil the beans in lightly salted water until *soft*. (I underline this as normally French beans are left crisp.)

Drain well. Make a purée in a blender or food processor.

Return the purée to the pan and over a low heat 'dry out' any excess water. Stir in the cream and butter. Check seasoning. Re-heat. Serve. Serves 4

### Pecorino, Cucumber, Tomato and Orange Salad with Anchovies

8 oz piece of Pecorino cheese, cut into cubes

2 beefsteak tomatoes, skinned, de-seeded and cut into ½ in. chunks

2 large navel oranges, peeled, segmented and cut into chunks

1 small cucumber, peeled, de-seeded and cut in half, then into ½ in. chunks

1 doz. anchovies, rolled, for garnish

*Dressing*

¼ pt olive oil

Juice and finely grated rind of one orange

1 tsp mild French mustard

Salt and milled pepper

1 clove garlic, crushed (optional)

1 tsp castor sugar

Put the dressing ingredients into a jar and shake well.

Mix the salad ingredients in a large bowl and put to chill.

Dress the salad just before serving. Garnish with the anchovies. Serves 6

### Winter Salad

2 green peppers

2 red peppers

2 Dill cucumbers

8 oz Gruyère, Emmenthal or Tôme de Brevis cheese, chilled

*Dressing*

¼ pt olive oil

2 tbsp white wine vinegar

1 level tsp mild French mustard

1 clove garlic, crushed

Salt and freshly milled pepper

*Garnish* (optional)
1 red skin onion, finely     1 tbsp freshly chopped
   sliced                        parsley

The secret of this salad is in the fine-cutting into strips of the peppers and cheese. Cut each pepper in half. Remove any seeds and pith, and cut away the stalk end.

Cut the halves into half again, and then laboriously shred each piece into fine striplets about $1\frac{1}{2}$ inches long. This is called a julienne, but if using a food processor use the *slicing* blade and *not* the julienne blade. It will look different but will be almost the same (the julienne blade of these machines doesn't work for peppers!). Cut the cucumbers into strips.

Chilling the cheese makes it easier to cut into same-sized strips as the peppers.

Store in separate containers. Mix together just before serving and toss in the dressing, which is made up in the usual way, just before your guests sit at table.

Peppers have a very strong flavour; this flavour 'crosses' between other food very quickly, and the idea is to keep the cheese flavour 'separate' from the peppers until the point of eating is reached.

Decorate with a few finely sliced onion rings and some freshly-chopped parsley. Serves 6